Minimalism

A Comprehensive Manual For Achieving A Simple And Purposeful Existence By Decluttering Your Living Space, Managing Your Finances, And Cultivating A Focused Mindset Minimalist Living & The Minimalist Budget

Emanuel Henriques

What Makes Something Minimalist?

For several reasons, it is quite beneficial to practice moderation. Some people engage in moderation because they are exhausted from owning so much "stuff." By all means, the benefits of possessing these items are outweighed by the cleaning, making up, fixing, and maintaining them. After relocating a few times, some people realized that many of their belongings were useless to transport. The most unnecessary items are those that are frequently never unpacked. A reduction in usage to benefit the environment. There is an enormous amount of garbage in our world, much of it completely unnecessary. Others just intend to start recognizing what is truly important by gathering their positive traits from daily life. Periodically, a strong shock is necessary, but many people realize that people come before stuff, and moderation helps to live this daily way of thinking.

These are just a few reasons you may want to begin or continue your adventure in moderation. You may be concerned about some of them or have a different reason entirely for appreciating moderation. Everybody has distinct motivations and methods of execution.

One person could not live without something that another believes to be unnecessary. This trip is largely dependent on you. There are no right or wrong answers in your quest to maintain a moderate lifestyle.

Many minimalists believe you should discard anything that isn't enjoyable or useful. Valuable things seem to be the clearest. You and everyone else in your home regularly utilize these items. It helps to apply moderation to your way of life while considering these basic concepts. You may claim, for instance, that you use all four cars, but would you need all four, or could you manage with only one? You will find stuff that you enjoy in the upcoming class. This could refer to anything that would make it truly amazing, truly delicious, or truly magnificent. This could include the most important souvenirs, memories, decorations, etc. Many minimalists will build three piles of stuff in each room. Excellent, valuable, and things that need to move somewhere are all included in the piles. Another room, a worthy purpose, something that can be bought, something that can be reused, or trash could be the intention somewhere. Later, this style might be useful while moving from room to room.

This book will help you navigate the several areas where you would like to implement a moderate lifestyle. Some of these ideas may resonate with you, while others may not. This book will help you liberate more time, space, energy, money, and limited resources.

You will probably notice that your life is somewhat more relaxed and enjoyable without unnecessary disruptions if you implement as many of these ideas as would be wise, followed by your portion. We will go room by room, space by space, and then expand to a few more commonplace, less significant issues where moderation may be beneficial. We ought to begin our goal by making a few minor adjustments.

Possible Benefits Of Living A Minimalist Lifestyle

More money; less money spent on unnecessary things; more energy available; less time spent on those unnecessary things

- More airy living areas

- Living areas are easier to clean
- Home migration is much easier

Time can be better spent reinforcing relationships with others, finding necessities more easily, worrying less about expensive stuff breaking or being stolen, having less debt, and, if wanted, being able to relocate to a more efficient, modest home.

These are but a few advantages of striving for a moderate lifestyle. Some of them might worry you, and some might not. Ideally, you see advantages that extend well beyond this list.

Using Simplicity In The Living Room

This could be your family room, lounge, or anything else you like. This is usually the first area guests see when they arrive at your house or where your family spends the most time getting to know one another. Many memories are formed there, so it's crucial to have the ideal amount of space and the items that are typically essential to everyone.

Your State Of Mind

Minimizing is pointless until you get your mentality in order. If you do and maintain the same attitude, you will quickly realize that your minimalism is futile since you have the mindset of someone who collects items, ideas, friendships, and memories. Since your attitude determines everything, let's start with clearing out your mentality.

Unbeknownst to you, internalized judgments are a major source of stress in your life. It doesn't matter if you don't live up to other people's expectations because everyone has opinions, some of which are invalid. Hence, you would discover that removing judgment from your outlook on life makes life easier and fosters greater empathy and compassion for others and yourself. How, then, do you eliminate the overabundance of ideas and the harmful mental patterns? Well, even medical professionals concur that practicing mindfulness is beneficial and simple.

After that, exhale to the count of ten. I want you to do this once a day for fifteen minutes or so. During that time, as you breathe, ideas will cross your mind. I want you to recognize that these people are there even though they aren't now your buddies. Although you can't completely avoid them, you can tell them that now is not the time for them to be there by removing judgment from the situation and dismissing their ideas. If you will, picture what you see through a train window. These are the ideas you have. They don't add feelings or opinions; they just appear one minute and disappear the next.

Being present in the breath and the moment is mindfulness's second facet.

What is meant by that? It means that you are not dwelling on the past since it is in the past and cannot be changed, nor are you concerned about it because it is still in the future. As a result, you reduce the entire mental process to what is going on right now. Consider the act of breathing in this manner to be the only thing occurring at that moment, but don't stop there.

When things bother you during the day, permit yourself to savor that moment. This entails using your senses—tasting the coffee, smelling the roses, and being alert. Although it may sound a bit unrealistic, practicing mindfulness can help you avoid overthinking everything that comes to mind and instead focus on getting things done. You must adopt this attitude as you purge items from your life and include things you cherish or find meaningful in your daily routine. It will take some time to form this habit, but once you do, you'll be glad you adopted a minimalist perspective. Try this every morning before the rest of the world wakes up, and then let your senses come alive once more during the day.

Chapter Four: The Tender and Challenging

My kids made a statement when they saw that there were fewer and fewer pictures of them on the dresser. They enjoyed seeing all of these nostalgic items that brought back memories of their childhood at home. However, I was unaware that they possessed the knowledge necessary to assist me in solving an issue. Each of them selected a single photo to hang on the walls of our house because I didn't want to dust the images constantly. Every other picture, greeting card, and keepsake was digitalized so we could view it whenever we wanted. Although I found it difficult to part with the originals, I packed them up and stored them in the loft for the kids to inherit in the future. The idea is that although sentimental items can be difficult to part with, you don't have to. In the digital age, all you have to do is transfer the photos to memory sticks, which most TVs will accept and use to show the pictures, saving you the trouble of constantly going through piles of rubbish and not losing anything.

There are further challenging items. People often give you things that you don't enjoy, but since it's your house and you're making a big minimalist design change, it's unlikely that they will notice if these objects disappear. People will notice that other items have dramatically replaced the gift and won't be disturbed that it no longer fits, supposing the inside of your house to be brand new. One aunt of mine gave me the most repulsive vase ever. It had been sent as a joke, and it seems that we had never really realized the hilarious side of it until she informed us, so she thought it was very funny that I had become brave enough to get rid of it.

Hold onto it if you adore it. Go ahead and use any other less-space-consuming methods of storing data that you have! Deprivation is not the goal of minimalism. It's about appreciating your existence and everything that clutters and adds unnecessary weight. You manage to break free from their hold gradually.

Specify the Final Look You Desire for Things: Consider the result before cleaning to clean effectively. You should have a place to make way. If the goal and the final product are not obvious, you won't be able to move on with other things.

Consider why a moderate home might benefit you if you have any interest in one. It suggests that providing a place to live satisfies the basic need for shelter. However, houses are much more than just places to hide out. They reflect who you are. The type of character you want your house to represent should be your top concern. Once that is evident, you want to arrange the items similarly. Assume that you need a place to work, play with your friends, express your creativity, and be comfortable at home. You'll be able to see your needs once that aspect is apparent. You can start preserving the items that help create that atmosphere and eliminate the ones that don't.

Attempting to incorporate all that into your house will lead to further chaos. It takes a lot of labor to alter everything and make it appear perfect. While some people are good at it, it doesn't assist in keeping the house organized or genuinely mess-free. It is constantly requested because there may be a need to deal with maintaining the setup going forward. It is a demanding and tiresome profession.

Utilise Your Resources As Best You Can

The technique of taking more work from the same resources is called minimalism.

To minimize your responsibilities and the amount of possessions in the household, you should concentrate on reducing their number. The number of things would increase if you had separate objects for every situation. This suggests a greater season of use, thorough cleaning, and additional spaces to store those items. It makes sense in the curious scenario where the items are non-replaceable. In any case, you should concentrate on using items with several uses. For example, choose clothing that can be used in multiple combinations, invest in kitchen appliances that can perform multiple tasks, and use a Swiss knife rather than an ordinary one to replace the little toolbox. Because they eliminate the need for separate items for small tasks, this assortment helps free up room in your house.

To improve the functionality of your house and advance your moderate plan, you need to find out how to implement this flexible usage design.

Adopt a Consistent Method

Cleaning is a never-ending task. Nobody ponders the passage of time. No matter how meticulous you were in cleaning, there would still be a mess. You would have to attempt things again and keep doing so again.

When you do it engagingly, the experience may become overwhelming. Long streaks of accumulation may be seen in one area, and sorting or tidying everything at once can be challenging. Here, your approach should be dependable. Avoid attempting to achieve everything at once. Start with a single area and go on gradually from there. Using this method will assist you in maintaining a mess-free and clean environment. You could choose to consistently maintain a neutral demeanor.

Stay Steady

The majority of the disarray we see in our houses, and ourselves is a result of our strong desires and aspirations. Even while it may seem wonderful to have lofty expectations or objectives, putting no effort into the ones you are not working for just leads to chaos. Placing the material in the middle of your lounge is fanciful, assuming you won't be a painter. You don't need the full sports equipment for casual walks that aren't too strenuous.

These kinds of things are messy. They drag down not just your wallet and house but also your soul. They would always evoke an urge or a ruined fantasy when you saw them. They don't even remotely assist you; instead, they keep you busy doing the things you enjoy. Being oriented around the important things is just as important as getting rid of the unnecessary things when practicing moderation.

As a result, eliminate everything that isn't helping you achieve your current goals. Get rid of the items saved for "in the event" scenarios. Reduce the surplus space in your closet and eliminate everything unnecessary to achieve your present objectives.

One Step at a Time, Please

Indeed, cleaning up things that have accumulated over a ten-year tendency is not an easy task. Your thinking mind will be your biggest enemy. You would be reminded that every item had some value when it was bought. Getting rid of stuff is a challenging scenario. Apart from that, cleaning is a difficult task in and of itself. It calls for planning and dedication. Nobody knows the true value of those things for you; thus, you are the only person who could do it.

Thus, start with a basic place. Choose the area in your house that needs cleaning quickly or the cleanest corner. You'll feel like you've accomplished something by doing this, and you'll also be able to see how much you can remove—even from areas that are cleaner than others. Organizing your space is not something that should be rushed. Understanding the true value of any object you keep or discard is important. You cannot take back the decisions you have made in the past. You ought to learn how to survive without the items you abandon.

Zen Tips for Decluttering: Developing a Minimalistic Attitude for a Clutter-Free Life

We must comprehend a Zen mind before looking at how to organize and modify one. Zen says that suffering comes from our connection to things and our expectations because we get upset if our expectations are not fulfilled and lose what we value but don't truly utilize. By adopting a Zen mindset, we might discover that happiness, contentment, and joy come from within ourselves rather than external sources. In today's society, we consider possessing more to be beneficial. But in the mentality of a Zen practitioner, less really is more. Thus, as you set out on your decluttering path, never forget that having fewer, more useful items taking up space and time is preferable to having an excess of unimportant items. Now that we know what Zen is about let's start decluttering. Decluttering can be daunting, particularly due to our emotional attachment to the things that make up most of our cluttered lives. When someone needs calm and quiet in their life but can't seem to get it elsewhere, what should they do? The organization is a good place to start, though. Organizing is organizing, just called differently. There are typically seven chronological steps to decluttering (which we will discuss briefly). We must discuss the minimalist attitude before we get to that section.

What is a minimalist mindset, and how does it connect to living a stress-free life and personal well-being? A minimalist is, in my opinion, someone who thinks that less is more. To put it plainly, this means that a minimalist seeks happiness by eliminating anything extra from their life to have a simpler, more contented life.

This seems untrue to some people. Some of us are so ingrained in our ideas and ways of thinking that we cannot imagine a life devoid of burdens and clutter. A minimalist decides to lead an unconventional life. He or she deliberately chooses to reduce life to its most necessities. Being minimal is not a way of life. It's more of an attitude. We do not need the luxuries we have today—such as automobiles, toys, and ten cell phones—to thrive. You undoubtedly question how it's possible if you can't imagine your existence without a smartphone. Living a minimalist lifestyle can help you live a simpler, clutter-free existence and help you pay off debt (many have done so). It has the power to grant you unfathomable freedom.

If you're enthused about the prospect, I'm sure you're eager to discover how to live a straightforward, clutter-free life. In what ways may a minimalistic mindset be used and adopted in an otherwise busy life? The solution is easy to understand. Adhere to the advice below.

How to Live a Minimal Life

You truly understand what matters in life when you lead a minimalistic lifestyle. If you take a moment to look at your house, you will find that there are many things you have either never used or used only once or twice over a long period. Has more application in daily life than in business. It claims that 80% of an effect results from 20% of the cause. You'll be shocked to hear that 80% of your life revolves around 20% of your activities and possessions if you closely examine the items you use in your daily life and around the house. Minimalism is a style of life and way of thinking encompassing much more than just living with the bare minimum of what makes you feel most comfortable. It extends beyond your living room, wardrobe, and drawers. Beyond all of this, it becomes a means of clearing your mind and delving even further into the primary source of your clutter. Eliminating anything that demands unnecessary time is a key component of minimalism. These are the actions you must take to adopt a minimalist lifestyle.

Step 1: Recognize and make a choice

Acknowledgment is the first step toward adopting a minimalist lifestyle and way of thinking. This is akin to your actions to break free from a certain vice. You must be honest about what you need and don't need at this step. To accomplish this:

Create a list.

Grab a pen and some paper.

Make a note of everything you own as you go around your house.

Once finished, sit and mark anything you haven't used in a while.

Moreover, remove everything you believe you won't need in the future. This list is beneficial since it gives you a clear understanding of how disorganized your life is. When I'm out shopping, I may use the list as a helpful benchmark by asking myself if I need what I will buy.

Step 2: Look for some inspiration

It's difficult to cultivate a minimalist mindset to the point where it permeates every aspect of your existence. It requires patience, a ton of practice, and bravery. It is, therefore, simple to become distracted and lose motivation when starting. Look for motivational factors to sustain your drive. Don't worry about how difficult it will be to put minimalist living into practice if you're doing it to keep organized and lower your stress levels. Think about how amazing it will feel to do the task successfully. Seek out inspiring ideas to strengthen your resolve.

Step 3: Get rid of whatever you don't need.

Now is the time to deal with the list we made in the first phase. Everything you crossed off the list should be deleted. Donate goods you don't need or use them for charity if you feel generous. Post things for sale if you feel like it.

Selling or donating whatever you haven't used in the last six months is a helpful tip. You can then proceed to 60 days after that. Don't forget to repeat the procedure.

Step Four: Repeat the procedure

Living simply is a way of life. You are not doing yourself any favors if you clear out clutter from your life today just to revert to your hoarding habits in a few months. Do you need this item? ask yourself before making a purchase." Am I able to live without this item? If the answer to this question is negative, return the item to the store because it will cause clutter in your house or area.

Step 5: Express gratitude for your efforts

Nothing is simple. When you reach your objectives, you frequently stop to recognize your hard work. The majority of us treat ourselves. Give yourself a small treat after three months of living a basic lifestyle. I'm not saying you have to go buy something you don't need; I'm just saying you should take a break. Spend a day off at the spar. Visit the golf course. Engage in a fun activity.

7. HOPE OF NOT MAKING IT:

Most individuals may fear missing something significant.

This concern arises from realizing all the products and pursuits in which a minimalist lifestyle would prevent us from engaging.

Beautiful images and videos of friends having fun can also be found online.

This may make it tough for you to keep to your minimalist lifestyle as you worry about missing out on something enjoyable.

8. MANIPULATION:

Some people may take the idea of materialism far too seriously.

They may strive to do everything the right way to improve their lifestyles, and even little deviations may upset them.

Artificial and unneeded pressure can impair rather than improve one's quality of life.

As a result, if you genuinely want to pursue the minimalist lifestyle, don't create unreasonable expectations for yourself to avoid feeling under pressure.

9. MINIMALISM ISN'T A SOLUTION TO ALL PROBLEMS:

As you may know, life is difficult, and maintaining a minimalist lifestyle would not instantly fix your problems.

Minimalism should be considered as a tool to offer you more time and mental ability to face your problems over time, which could lead to better contentment with life in the long run.

10. ISSUES WITH THE MIND:

Some people may find it challenging to change to a minimalist lifestyle in a mentally healthy way.

A minimalist lifestyle may not be the greatest option for them because it might lead to serious mental health concerns.

Many people may experience unhappiness, despair, or other mental health concerns as a result of a strong attachment to their materialistic lifestyle.

11. A MINIMALIST LIFESTYLE IS DIFFICULT TO MAINTAIN FOR FAMILIES:

Establishing a minimalist lifestyle can be tough, especially if you have children.

Parents routinely purchase pricey toys and other stuff for their children.

As a result, your child may anticipate you to do the same and may be dissatisfied if he or she does not receive the products and toys that he or she desires as a surprise gift.

As a result, you may not want to upset your child and, sooner or later, make compromises to your minimalist lifestyle.

12. YOU'RE NOT READILY IMPRESSED AND DON'T SUFFER FROM THE AFFLICTION OF "SHINY THING DISORDER":

It could appear to be an advantage, but the fact is that many things lose their shine and brilliance over time, and there are risks of being unhappy.

The Ancient Greeks

There are two old sayings, and they are:

(1) Those who forget history lessons are bound to repeat them.

(2) There is nothing new beneath the sun.

From about 400 BC to 300 BC, the ancient Greeks studied numerous ideas that held the essence of consumerism and minimalism. The philosophies that I regard as forerunners of these were hedonism as the predecessor of consumerism and either Epicureanism or Stoicism as the forerunners of minimalism.

Hedonism

Hedonists think pleasure and utility are the same and that pleasure governs all human beings and is the main aim in life. Hedonists say that there are just two things that inspire human action.

These are pleasure and pain; decisions should aim to boost our comfort and lessen or fully eliminate discomfort. This is a definition of those who believe in consumerism without disdain for the future due to mass manufacturing, which, of course, the Greeks of those times had no means of understanding.

Epicureanism

Epicureanism is practiced by Epicureans who also feel that pleasure is essential. Still, the best means of attaining pleasure is by living a humble life, enriched by learning a knowledge of the world and a limit being placed on one's wishes. If this route is pursued, one reaches a condition of peace, security, and a lack of physiological suffering. This is simply a minimalist philosophy.

Stoicism

Stoicism is practiced by stoics who think that happiness for humans is gained by acceptance of one's situation in life, consciously not being under the influence of our yearning for pleasure or dread of suffering. Like the epicureans, they believe that it is preferable to acquire knowledge of the world, understand and play our role in nature's plan, and be fair and just to others.

It is debatable whether this is a minimalist philosophy. Minimalists do not mindlessly accept the world as it is. They consciously reject the mindset of the consumerist and his or her hedonistic lifestyle, which is viewed as a tremendous threat to the world, particularly the one that their children and grandkids will have to live in.

That completes our discussion of what minimalism is and what it is opposed to. The subsequent chapters will discuss minimalist approaches to housing, eating, decluttering, and living.

Chapter 2: 20 + 1 Minimalism Tips

Write Down Your Reasons for Minimalism and T0-do List

Making a rundown isn't an issue for some. But for others, it may not be why they desire to become a minimalist. Make a summary of why you need to go for moderation. A part of the causes may be feeling less anxious, setting aside cash, having more opportunities to appreciate family, or having an excellently coordinated home. It is vital to begin considering an objective and set up an arrangement. Having an arrangement benefits you by remaining on track. Record every one of the regions you need to clean up or every one of the rooms you need to coordinate, then pick the first on your rundown whenever you have determined that, then find a space inside that room and begin to get rid of everything.

As for daily agendas, writing every one of the missions you wish to complete provides you with an unmistakable notion of what you need to do, and you would then break down the endeavorsinto more moderate advancements, making them simpler to accomplish. If your standard daily schedule is as long as your arm, set yourself to do less. Begin to develop a rundown and compose your three Most Important Things, otherwise called MIT's, for the afternoon. Whenever you have done those, go to your unique rundown and pick a thing to do, supplied that you have a chance and willpower. In any case, accomplishing your MITs is vital because they are your fundamental and most significant tasks.

Simplify Your Morning Routine

Start your day as you mean to continue and improve on it. This is the way you can accomplish it.

Don't Press Snooze: Don't hit the snooze when the morning alarm goes off because ten extra minutes won't make much difference. Get off your bed when the alarm goes off, and you will have a better, more efficient start to your day.

Get a shower timer: Invest in a shower timer. It will help you use less water, time, and energy.

Automate your morning coffee: If morning coffee is a must, invest in a programmable coffee machine. The machine will fix you quickly and could make a difference in your day.

Sort your clothes the night before. Sorting your clothes the night before will help you avoid wasting crucial time.

Go for a cold breakfast if you are in a hurry: Don't start cooking if you are in a hurry. Focus on fruit salad, yogurt, cereal, or granola and minimize time spent on rush morning hours.

Set a countdown timer: For example, you may have to leave the house for 40 minutes. So, set a countdown timer to keep track of time.

Leave yourself notes: Don't rely only on your memory power to remember things. Leave yourself notes to make things easier for yourself.

Utilize your commute: If you use a private car, you can use the time to eat breakfast on the way to work. If you use a bus or train, then use the time to check social sites, email, and read the news. Or you can use the time to meditate.

Decide On the Value of Your Items

To carry on with a moderate life, you want to settle on the worth of your things. Ask yourself inquiries such as:

Would you have to purchase the item again at the original price?

If someone gives you the item, would you keep it? Does the item remind you of your happy memories?

Minimalism isn't tied in with disposing of pointless stuff. It is tied in with concluding which things carry more worth to your life. Here is a rundown of times you should get freed:

Old magazines

Clothes that don't fit

Half-finished craft projects Chipped or cracked crockery Book you have never read and won't ever read

Pens that don't work

Out-of-date foods in the cupboards Baby items that don't have any use Old bedding

Anything that makes you feel sad or guilty

Jigsaws are games that are missing some pieces

Anything that doesn't work

Extra mugs and glasses Educational notes

Tights with ladders

CDs, DVDs

Cushions/pillows

Recipe books that you don't use Old nail varnish

Dead plants/flowers

VHS tapes and audio cassettes Excess furniture

Out-of-date clothes

Out-of-date newspapers

Old calendars and diaries

Sports equipment no longer used

Anything in your car that doesn't provide value

Cuddly toys are no longer needed. Set Up A Clutter Donation Box now

Artwork that doesn't make you happy

Large items that take up too much room

Scraps of wrapping paper

Specialist tea/coffee you never drink

Old computers

Out-of-date medicines

Memorabilia that doesn't hold the same value now

Unneeded bits of paper/receipts Bad photos

Junk mail

Shoes that hurt

Ornaments

Greeting cards from past events Excess baking trays/ pans

Used candles

Kids artwork

Outside furniture

Excess loose change

Anything waiting to be returned

Bottles of alcohol

Setting up a messiness gift box can assist you with wiping out the mess from your home. This pack, box, or bushel ought to be a decent component of your home since it will assist you with wiping out the mess from your home regularly.

Empty the case routinely. You can do it by selling the things or giving the things to your loved ones who could utilize them. Additionally, you can set up a few boxes.

For this procedure to work, you can assemble and name boxes

The keep put away box: This book will be the smallest in theory. You only place items that are used on a daily or weekly basis.

The donate/sell box: This box will be filled with items you don't use. Regardless of its condition, donating everything you don't need is tempting.

The toss box: As the name suggests, you keep items you need to eliminate.

The storage box: Think twice before placing items in this box because it can quickly cause clutter. The seasonal clothing or décor are the items suited for this box.

Store Things Organized and Out of Sight

Here is the manner by which you can do it

Kitchen

Go through your pots, dishes, and utensils and dispose of additional items and copies. Pass

the additional things to another person or give them away. Do likewise with any remaining things in your kitchen and make kitchen cupboards more organized.

Use glass compartments or transparent plastic holders in the cooler to assist your family with knowing what food varieties are available.

Bathroom

Use dividers or small baskets to make the most of the available drawer space.

Divide items by use. For example, place tooth care and cosmetics in separate baskets.

Arrange extra bottles of shampoo, skin, and body care products in an orderly fashion on a shelf to avoid buying additional items.

Buy a small caddy for each person in your home. Tell each person to place their shampoo, conditioner, razor, or other items in the caddy.

Bedrooms

Buy an appropriate size dresser for your clothing and avoid stuffing them fully.

Living Area and Dining Room

Buy a bin or a small basket for everyone in your family. Label them with names and stack them in the living or dining room corner. Go through the dining and living space daily and place items in the appropriate bin. Each family member is responsible for returning their items to the appropriate bin. Garage

Install shelves on the wall of your garage and keep the floor clutter-free. Avoid cardboard boxes for storing items. Use labeled or clear plastic bins to store items in an organized way.

Install ceiling and pegs or wall hooks to store tools, sports equipment, and bikes.

The Benefits Of Simple Living

Living simply voluntarily is not the goal of voluntary simplicity. To live in balance is to set higher standards. This is a moderate approach that straddles the extremes of luxury and poverty. -Duane Elgin

There are many advantages to minimalism that outweigh the minimalist. Its overall simplicity and avoidance of complexity positively impact various topics, including psychology, spiritual development, health, emotions, and a host of other topics. A handful of them consist of:

Benefits to Health

Removing stress significantly impacts a person's ability to heal from past trauma, gives them morhealthilyise, and generally detaches themselves from their material life.

Financial Advantages

Reducing the excess burden of commitments and engagements can significantly boost one's finances, ensure prudent investment spending, and increase skyrocketing savings. A person's financial life will be positively impacted by changing their schedule in more ways than one, as plenty of engagements equate to plenty of money.

It fosters creativity.

It's startling yet accurate. One of the unique characteristics that distinguished the Israelites as philosophers and children of God was that, given their early history as meek and unrefined mud bearers, they had ample opportunity for philosophical reflection, appreciation of nature, and frequent encounters with God. This fact is practically recorded in the majority of the Bible's stories. Imagine King David and Solomon penning one or two books in the Bible. Even though they were kings, they had a lot of time. The Bible contains five opening books written by the Prophet Moses. This was a stark contrast to their Gentile neighbors, whose lives were characterized by engagements, feasts, idolatry, celebrations, and revelry—not to mention evil. The number of engagements was so great that even the idols they worshipped could not spend enough time with them.

Improved Bonds

Not that one doesn't have relationships with people when their schedule and activities are packed full of activities and appointments. However, the desire to dazzle others with flashy mobile phones, cutting-edge vehicles, astute clothing, and other accouterments of contemporary life is ingrained in that. Relationships are automatically healed and function better when decluttering takes place. Additionally, there is a tendency to pay better and more attention to the items and gadgets we don't need, and many things work better in a decluttered life.

Contribution to Society: Any individual whose life isn't organized will frankly acknowledge that most common aspects of this life are rooted in a neurotic tendency. When life becomes uncluttered, one's focus and attention are transferred from oneself to others. This is one of the numerous reasons why most religious affiliations disapprove of overindulgence in material possessions such as jewelry, beauty and makeup, money and love, and the rest. These things aren't seen appropriately until the system is thoroughly audited and lightened.

Evaluate How You Spend Your Time.

There's a widespread misperception that minimalism is exclusively about material goods. In actuality, clutter is more than just stuff. Activities that frequently squander valuable time may be the culprit. Because of this, evaluating how you spend your time and identifying the things that contribute to your priorities in life—as well as those that don't—will be necessary steps in your journey towards minimalism.

Consider the following questions as you consider your daily routine: Does this activity improve my life, and if yes, how much? If the first question is "no," then it is obvious that this kind of activity has to stop. If you responded "yes" to the first question and "not much" to the second, there's a strong likelihood that it will also need to end.

You put yourself in a position to free up more time for activities that add much value to your life. In the unlikely event that you find a lot of activities that should be stopped, I strongly advise concentrating on stopping one of these activities at a time, giving the most importance to the ones that waste the most time. If you eliminate them all immediately, you might become overwhelmed and give up on the quest.

Evaluate Your Connections

Surprise! Relationships are a big part of minimalism, staff, and activities! You see, relationships can either make it easier for you to achieve your goals or prevent you from doing so. There's such a thing as "relationship clutter" as well, and to truly keep your life joyful, deeply fulfilling, and simple, you need to keep the relationships that can support you in that endeavor and let go of the ones that can't.

I'm not advocating that you start evaluating the personalities of the people you interact with. This isn't the point about that. Recall that everything revolves around living in harmony with the most important things in your life. It won't involve making moral or immoral character judgments about individuals. It will entail deciding whether or not your relationships with individuals are advancing your prioritized list so that you can spend more time with those who are. You see, it comes down to evaluating the outcomes of your relationships with particular individuals rather than their personalities.

Proceed cautiously and one step at a time, just as you would with eliminating unnecessary pursuits and items. Relationships are probably the hardest to end because they entail feelings and emotional attachments. Concentrate on one relationship at a time, progressively cutting back on your interactions with specific people until you can stop communicating with them regularly.

Set Boundaries

Living a minimalist lifestyle involves acknowledging that certain things, activities, or relationships may not be entirely avoidable or removed because they don't align with your priorities. Consider the Internet, particularly if you work as a freelancer online. Limitations rather than total elimination will be the optimal minimalist strategy for such items.

Returning to the Internet example, you can restrict your use to a certain time frame, such as during your lunch break and the first hour after work, i.e., only from 5 to 6 p.m., even though it's probably not practical to give it up entirely. In this manner, you can take a break before heading home and check your email for important messages. Limiting your exposure can lessen the clutter that going online can bring into your life.

One Item at a Time

I apologize for shattering your illusion, but multitasking is a myth. And no, computers cannot multitask; instead, they simply switch between tasks at such rapid speeds that it gives the impression that they can handle many tasks simultaneously. Shifting attention from one task to another is what many mistake for multitasking.

Within the framework of minimalism, multitasking should be avoided because it leads to mental clutter, which is a different kind of clutter. Working on several projects at once can cause your mind to become cluttered, making it difficult for you to concentrate fully on the task at hand. Furthermore, you risk performing a task poorly when you cannot, which increases the likelihood that you will have to spend more time fixing errors or redoing tasks.

And when making the switch to a minimalist lifestyle, I strongly advise getting rid of one unnecessary item at a time. This will enable you to give it your all when parting with a non-essential item from your life, which can greatly improve your chances of success. Additionally, as you eliminate more items from your life, you'll feel more confident that you can successfully minimize your life, making subsequent eliminations much simpler.

Little Steps

Permit me to restate what I wrote: They were busy laying bricks by the hour, but Rome wasn't built in a day.

Changing to a minimalist lifestyle will require consistency and time, much like building Rome. Your chances of successfully switching to a minimalist lifestyle will be the only thing you minimize if you try to do it quickly by taking just a few significant steps.

Why? It's because major life changes are difficult and intimidating. On the other hand, baby steps are much simpler, and the more you consistently complete tasks, the more motivated and confident you will feel about your ability to succeed. So attempt to tackle one room at a time rather than clearing everything extra in your house. Additionally, concentrate on one or two smaller sections of the room simultaneously while going room by room.

Lead a Purposeful Life

Intentional living, or the capacity to live in the present and do so on purpose rather than by accident, is another aspect of minimalism. When you live intentionally, you take control of your lifestyle instead of letting your surroundings and circumstances dictate it.

Living in the present, which involves being conscious of it and not dwelling on the past or future, is crucial. For instance, when you're having dinner with your significant other on your anniversary, try not to think about the work you failed to finish earlier in the day or the work you have to finish tomorrow. Enjoy the celebration and avoid letting your thoughts be consumed by things you cannot change at that precise moment. In the Bible, Jesus Christ said to let tomorrow worry about itself.

I'm not suggesting that you ignore the past and fail to draw any lessons from it—especially from your mistakes. Putting aside irrelevant thoughts about past mistakes or shortcomings and learning from them at a later time is what I mean when I talk about being in the moment. It can be difficult to enjoy the present and create new, beautiful things when your mind is cluttered with thoughts of the past and the future.

Intentional living gives you complete control over your surroundings and circumstances—rather than vice versa. When you can do this, you'll be able to manage the amount of clutter in your life and lead a more fulfilling existence. Living a minimalist lifestyle requires you to live very differently from the rest of the world because minimalism contradicts the worldly grain of materialism. You must take charge of your life, clear out as much clutter as possible, and direct it toward your priorities.

7 Ways To Try Living On Less

1. apparel. Statistics show that we wear 20% of our garments 80% of the time. This implies that many of us own closets full of clothing that neither fits nor enjoys. They are simply taking up space. The straightforward exercise of going through your closet and removing unnecessary clothing makes. Give your lighter wardrobe 30 days to do its work, and you won't miss those out-of-date clothes.

2. Decorations. Many of the decorations in our homes are not meaningful to us personally. Unfortunately, they distract you and your guests from the décor in your home that tells your story and accentuates your qualities. Take a

moment to examine your house with a critical eye. Take only those decorations that are the most meaningful and beautiful. Your house will start telling your story in a lovely way. Additionally, your previous decorations will probably end up at your next garage sale.

3. Games. All too frequently, we let ourselves get into the mindset that "more is better," and our children follow suit. We start buying and gathering too many toys for our kids. Our children don't need to learn to be creative, helpful, caring, or share. Thus, your children may benefit from having fewer toys in various ways. Even if you might want to consult your children before moving their used toys, there's a good

chance that the old, used toys will be lost in a matter of weeks (unless someone used to pick them all up).

4. Cooking Utensils. Our kitchens don't seem to have enough storage space, though. However, compared to many of us now, most of our grandmothers cooked far more frequently, inventively, and far better—in significantly smaller kitchens. The truth is that simplicity is almost always preferable when it comes to cooking. We require significantly fewer cooking tools than we now have. Therefore, if we simply owned the drawers, cabinets, and countertops, they could be far more organized and functional.

5. Televisions. Furthermore, there are currently more television sets in American homes than people. Over the previous two years, that barrier had decreased. The typical home has 2.55 persons and 2.73 TV sets. A television set is used for more than a third of the day in the average American home— eight hours and fourteen minutes, to be exact. We are watching life pass us by while we sit on the curb. Try your hand at owning smaller televisions. As a result, you will observe lesions. When you do, as a family, you will be more eager to do it.

6. Countertops. Clutter is a type of distortion. It draws our attention and refocuses our thoughts, even for a

moment. Anything that is arranged on your counters is vying for your attention. Unfortunately, we have grown so accustomed to these distractions that we hardly even notice them until they are removed. Try it, even if it's just for a week, and ensure your counterpoints are crystal clear. Place items in drawers, cabinets, pantries, or temporary storage boxes. For convenience's sake, you'll probably return part of it after a week, but I'm willing to wager that you won't return the entire amount.

7. Pieces of furniture. Removing excess furniture from your rooms can require heavy lifting, but if you're up for the challenge, it will instantly create significant space and airflow in your

home. The seldom-used furniture pieces in your house are easily recognizable and occupy more space than you think. Yes, this experience requires a location to store your furniture throughout the trial period, but it's a quick and simple way to eliminate some of the biggest Clutter in your house.

Chapter Four: Cutting Down on Your Purchasing

You'll find that every time you go shopping, you buy things you didn't plan to. While you might think it's smart to start looking for possible Christmas gifts in June, it's not that smart. Your priorities will have shifted by the time Christmas rolls around, just like they do for other people. To start saving for Christmas, just take the money you save each week for your shopping and put it into a bank account. This way, you'll have extra cash to buy Christmas gifts for family and friends. Examine the upcoming shopping load in your cart and arrange your purchases on a table. After dividing them into several heaps, you'll be shocked to learn the truth about your purchasing behaviors.

Step 4: Arrange your groceries.

These heaps ought to be labeled:

Essentials

unhealthy snacks

wholesome meals

Extras that are not necessary

Nobody is advocating that you must purchase something at a discount. You can get the highest-quality goods if you are prudent in your business dealings. For instance, when you can prepare the food and know exactly what's in it, why feed your children manufactured garbage? When you know it's not a healthy method to feed your family, why pay extra just because the manufacturer packed it and persuaded you to buy it? There's no longer a justification for prepackaged foods with additives and preservatives. With all of the appliances available these days, all you would have needed to do to make a delicious, homemade stock pot stew was to put all the ingredients in a slow cooker the night before. Using an air fryer is another way to cook without using any fat. When you do, you'll discover that your food is healthier and requires less time to prepare. Furthermore, there is less cleanup for you to complete. After installing an air fryer, I've noticed that I use the oven less frequently and don't need to consume as much fat overall.

Now, examine the optional extras.

These are the items that enticed you to purchase. Maybe they were positioned in a certain store area to entice you to buy them. Experts have figured out the psychology of store layout, and if you let them, they will always take advantage of you. Making a grocery list and sticking to it is a habit that you have to get into.

Although it could seem like it turns shopping into a nuisance, in the end, you bring less Clutter into your house, making it easier to maintain and more pleasurable to live in.

Step 5: Shopping for clothing

You likely have a closet full of items you rarely wear. The amount of clothing you must sort through daily to find that perfect outfit is why you have difficulty finding anything. Before shopping for clothes, you need to organize your wardrobe; we will discuss that in the upcoming chapter. For now, try to reduce your shopping by convincing yourself that you don't need the item you are considering purchasing unless you are positive it would improve your life. The idea that these are options rather than necessities is one of the hardest concepts to comprehend when surrounded by consumer-pleasing stores and television ads. Even though you may have an obsession with shoes, it is useless to hunt for new additions to your collection until you are certain of what you own for every situation. Minimizing entails using a reasonable strategy. You can certainly own a pair of shoes if they bring you joy, but consider whether the joy will last only till you wear them once or whether they will truly contribute something useful to your wardrobe that will bring you joy every day. You likely buy things impulsively, so your wardrobe is probably overflowing with items. Impulsive buying rarely works.

Being minimalist does not imply deprivation. It implies that having less equates to more. You can now afford that gorgeous designer clothing you've always desired. But if you want it, what are you willing to part with to make room in your closet for it?

Chapter 4: The House of Minimalism

Every little thing in a minimalist home has a purpose, which makes it beautiful. Because maintaining it is nearly straightforward, it is also tidy, well-maintained, and organized. Furthermore, because it contains the items the homeowner values most, a minimalist home captures the essence of the homeowner's personality.

You can take pleasure in owning a simple house, too. You may turn your house into one by following these two easy steps. The first is decluttering, and the second is making your house more straightforward.

First Step: Clear Out Clutter

The minimalist philosophy emphasizes how important it is to clear Clutter because it wastes time and creates stress. The cost of organizing Clutter also includes purchasing storage items and the time and money needed to maintain them. It will be well spent, even though clearing Clutter takes time. It's crucial to rid your house of everything superfluous because doing so symbolizes mental clarity.

Modify your perspective. Creating a mindset of "That's enough" rather than "What else can I buy?" is the first step towards decluttering your home. Learn to let go of the need to hoard, primarily for sentimental reasons and the fear of losing material belongings. Remember that these are just objects and that giving them away to people who are in greater need of them than you is a better way for them to fulfill their intended function.

Throw away anything that hasn't been utilized in more than six months. You likely no longer need an item if it hasn't captured your interest. You may occasionally consider the possibility that you MIGHT require it in the future. Sadly, this notion is a justification to hold onto your stuff.

If you are unsure whether to discard a certain item, consider the following: "Have I used this in the last six months?" When might I use this again if I don't donate it or throw it away? Will I be able to rent, borrow, or buy a new one if I need to donate or discard this one? Nevertheless, since you haven't used it in over six months, the likelihood that you would ever need it again is very low. For seasonal goods, like winter apparel, you can extend the period to a full year.

Snap pictures of cherished objects. An item typically has sentimental value because of the memories associated with it, not only because it is housed in the home. If the objects are old photos or documents, scan them into your computer and let them go so the memories can be preserved without taking up physical space. Try this with a few old treasured items and see how you feel afterward. It could seem daunting at first.

Maintain a "maybe" bucket. While you continue to declutter your home, if there are some things you just can't bring yourself to part with for the time being, you can keep them together in one bin. Make a note of the things in the box and schedule a follow-up reminder for six months from now so you have time to decide.

Separate and conquer. Every day, set aside a short period to organize your house, one area at a time. You might begin by focusing on the main features in each space, including the bed, bookcase, and kitchen sink. After taking everything out of one area, divide the items into three piles: store (in your "maybe" container), throw (or donate), and keep. After that, place the objects in the "keep" pile back in that area. Just be sure to apply it after giving the area a good cleaning.

Step 2: Make your house simpler

You might need some time to adjust to living in a minimalist house, but in the end, you'll be happy you made a move. However, keeping up with household maintenance and creating the proper habits to minimize duties requires discipline and work.

It would be helpful to have an idea of the typical design of a minimalist home to create a minimalist system for housekeeping. The following are some attributes you should strive for:

Pieces of furniture that are necessities. The only objects in any area are truly utilized, not just decorative pieces. A minimalist kitchen, for instance, might contain a sink, stove, refrigerator, and a shelf to accommodate the same amount of pottery as the occupants.

Clean surfaces. Except for a few necessary items like a light or a container of flowers, if it makes you happy, flat surfaces like floors and tables are usually clear. Nor even a pile of books or papers or other random trinkets.

Gentle, harmonious hues. The fundamentals will shine out in a room when simple colors are used. White, for example, has long been a classic minimalist mainstay because it elongates small spaces and is such a calming color that you can relax and decompress just by gazing at it. Of course, in addition to white, you may also go with other muted hues like green, beige, and blue.

Thoughtful accents. While the main goal of minimalism is to maintain the necessities, you may still appreciate the artwork and vibrant colors. You may, for example, leave much of your wall empty save for a framed family portrait or an original painting. Additionally, you can add accent pieces to your home to create a cozier atmosphere, such as a crimson pillow with your plain white couch or a potted plant.

Every object has a location. Maintenance will be simple if you assign a specific location for everything you own. Since you will have fewer things, keeping them all organized will not be difficult. Ensure that the products are arranged in the best locations for you. For instance, keep items you use regularly handy and store items you use infrequently on a shelf or in a drawer.

Your property doesn't need to become a minimalist residence overnight. On the other hand, you can use your intense desire for this change as motivation to simplify, clean, rearrange, and declutter. Ultimately, what matters most is feeling comfortable, secure, and happy in your own house.

They provide real-world examples that material possessions, wealth, and happiness are not always the keys to a fulfilling existence.

They are the live embodiment of the opposite of the Industrial Revolution philosophy that Schumacher championed: greater does not always equal better.

Even now, these men continue to teach that they made the right decision. They have stated to numerous individuals and media outlets that they have achieved a balance in their lives that their wealth could not provide, and they cannot recall a period in which they were happier.

Yes, I am aware of this. As your mounting debt nags at the back of your mind, you sit there staring at the screen of your phone, wondering what psychological disorder they would be suffering from to support this way of thinking. However, I can guarantee you that no aberrant psychological condition is present.

So, how do you maintain your minimalist spirit in a possessive world? Following the six main principles of a minimalist lifestyle—less is more, getting rid of unnecessary items, living in the present, scheduling your time, discovering your purpose, and putting yourself first—is the first step. By adopting and using these six fundamental principles, you will learn how to shift your attention from external incentives to internal motivation.

There are external motivators all around us:

You work hard to get a promotion.

You work late at night to avoid getting fired.

You exercise and follow a diet to shed pounds to enjoy your favorite cake for the celebration.

People who voluntarily abstain from profiting from an external motivator are all around us. This hinders many people's ability to be motivated internally, wherein one's desire to accomplish something and their own satisfaction originate from within. You become less vulnerable to mishaps and unexpected meetings that stress you out since you have more time to fit them in when you learn effective time management techniques. By focusing on yourself, you may go deeper and uncover your true desires rather than cover them up with social pressures in an attempt to save money and accomplish them now rather than putting them off till later.

You will demonstrate to yourself how fulfilling this lifestyle can be by emphasizing the idea of getting rid of the unwanted and how pointless many of the items you have bought actually are. More than any other aspect of the philosophy, this can provide insight into the validity of leading a simple life.

Your life can be changed by minimalism in ways you may not even be aware of.

Section 3: How Minima

Attaining Relationship Minimalism

This is the most significant and vital stage in adopting a minimalist lifestyle.

Relationships with friends, family, kids, spouse, or partner are extremely important. Maintaining these ties is vital, but you must also recognize the partnerships that impede your progress and prevent you from reaching your ultimate objectives.

Alongside Family and Kids

Spending less time with your family, friends, and kids does not imply that you are being minimalistic with them. To make them feel loved, valued, and cared for, you have to offer them a significant amount of your everyday attention and prioritize them.

But you also have to point them to simplicity and teach them its significance. Explain to them the benefits of simplicity for both of you. Instruct them to:

- Getting more stuff isn't the path to happiness
Being unique in one's life is quite acceptable.
- It's a smart idea to consider your purchases carefully.
- Living intelligently means staying within your means.
- Caring is sharing.
- Clutter is only a burden.
- It's critical to regulate your wants about objects
- Family needs to come first, above all else.

Thanks to these beliefs, they will be able to live a simpler life and abstain from pointless actions.

With Pals

This category is quite expansive. Most of us have developed the bad habit of calling everyone we meet for two days "friends." You should stop doing this. It's time you realized that there is a difference between an acquaintance and a friend.

Your true friends are The folks who help, support, and encourage you. People who inspire you to be positive and constructive and who help you achieve your goals. These individuals are your network of support and will be invaluable to you.

Many more folks are in your immediate vicinity besides those who don't assist you. Instead, they squander your time, depress and demoralize you, encourage you to engage in harmful behaviors and divert your attention from your goals. You must get rid of these individuals from your life. Start removing these individuals from your social circle to declutter it.

Do make friends, but only those who will love and support you no matter what. To move forward in the right route, you must cut off those linked to you with hidden agendas.

How To Simplify Your Goals For Your Career And Work

Living a minimalist lifestyle regarding your relationships, relationships, furniture, clothes, and utilities is just one aspect of decluttering your life. It is a style of life guided by contented and uncomplicated living. As such, it encompasses all aspects of you, including your ideas, activities, aspirations, and professional goals.

Make Your Goals and Thoughts Simpler

Simplifying your ideas and end goals is the first step towards implementing minimalism in your professional and business goals. Reflect on your long-term objectives and the concepts brewing when you are alone. You should eliminate negative ideas if you discover they are predominately present in your head. Meditation and yoga are the finest ways to get rid of negativity. If you become friends with them, you won't ever need to struggle with negative ideas again. They will come into your life, but you can eliminate them.

Second, you must justify your objectives. Determine the viability and attainability of the goals you have set for yourself. If not, consider making them simpler or doing away with them if you work too hard to complete them. You can simplify your professional life and job aspirations as soon as your goals are narrowed down.

Streamlining Your Goals and Professional Life

You should proceed to achieve minimalism in your work life and ambitions after you have streamlined your thoughts and objectives. Do you often work past office hours to accomplish your ultimate goals? Do you work extra hours to make more money or do an office job in your spare time? If so, you should stop doing these workouts.

Working as little as possible to support yourself and not rely on others is what it means to be a minimalist. You would only need a decent amount of money because you would already have streamlined various parts of your life.

You must so cease doing all the extra effort and part-time work you are doing. Instead, make the most of that time by working on yourself, unwinding, and getting to know your family and kids.

Your stress level will significantly decrease if you take it easy in your work life. Making a lot of money would no longer be a problem for you, and removing this extra load would result in a fantastic transformation in your life—you would begin to lead a serene life. Furthermore, your relationship with your family will deepen, and they won't complain about your carefree attitude toward them.

Chapter 4: Making Your Home Smaller

How Your Home Can Be Minimized

Here are some ideas for incorporating minimalism into your house to make it more amazing and memorable.

Vacuum and sweep your home in phases.

Try not to tackle your house's decluttering all at once. That will be stressful, and if you must get through a lot of stuff at once, you could reconsider adopting a minimalist lifestyle. Go slowly and steadily to make sure you don't give up on your aim of being a minimalist. Cleaning and sweeping your home in waves is an effective technique.

Grab a box and explore your house room by room. Take ten minutes to go through each room and fill your box with everything you no longer use or need.

Staples you haven't used in years should go in that box if sitting in your study area. Include the scarf in that box if you've outgrown it.

After finishing the first wave:

Move on to the second.

Pay close attention to all the duplicates you rarely use or enjoy this time.

Get rid of the other two pairs of jeans if you own four, but only wear two.

Take out the plates if you use very few, yet your kitchen cupboard has too many that take up too much room.

Proceed to the third wave after completing the second, and examine your rooms, closets, wardrobes, and cupboards in great detail. Get rid of everything that is not essential to you anymore, including additional furniture, silverware, clothes, accessories, makeup, kitchenware, toiletries, toys, and books. Save everything you truly utilize, have sentimental value for you, and tell a tale about you. For example, hold onto the blue ottoman your great-grandfather gave you for Christmas and the gold medal you won in your first 100-meter run. These items give your home personality and meaning.

You don't need to complete all three waves in a single day. They can be dispersed over several days or even weeks. Take as much time as necessary to declutter your home because the goal is to make it a pleasurable and meaningful task that will motivate you to maintain minimalism in the long run.

Organize and Clean Your Home

Once your entire house has been decluttered, tidy and arrange everything, dust everything before using a mop to clean the sticky floor or items. After your home is spotless, arrange everything in a tidy manner. Your home will begin to look cozier and friendlier than before.

Make a Space Free of Clutter

Make a space free of clutter in your home to become motivated to live with far less than you believe you need. This area should never be cluttered to serve as a constant reminder of your pledge to lead a simple life and find contentment in owning fewer, more meaningful possessions.

Your nightstand, closet, study room table, or living room cupboard could all be clutter-free. Keep this area clutter-free at all times, and use it as motivation to make the rest of your home clutter-free.

Use your diary to record your feelings as you implement these changes in your home. This enables you to monitor your progress and record your feelings regarding minimalism. Examine your emotions frequently to keep track of your progress and any errors you may have made.

Apply minimalism to your relationships and family after implementing it in your home. How to achieve that is covered in the next chapter.

Chapter 3: The Method of Decluttering

There are numerous applications for your trash to be useful. Maybe there are other options, or maybe you want a garage sale to remove part of the stuff.

Locations for the destitute

Giving instructional materials to schools, giving to relatives, Binding

You should bring enough big black bags and labels when you begin, room by room, to mark anything removed from the room and prevent it from being unintentionally given away. Putting away, selling, and giving are some names for them. That will assist you in organizing the things in the rooms, but there might be larger items you wish to market for sale, or that need to be transported to businesses. If so, remove them from the room and keep them in the garage so you can remove them and free up your space for whatever will be occupying it. The notion is to never leave a room unfinished. Everything needs to be evaluated, including the floor and the ceiling. This applies to all items in your home—drapes, photographs, decorations, rugs, and more—because clutter reduces your house's space. A room will appear larger the more natural light it receives. The space will appear larger and more airy with less pattern on the walls and carpeting. As a result, you must establish and adhere to your priorities. The most amazing Persian rugs were in one of the houses I worked on, but there was so much garbage that you could hardly see them.

And on top of that, they were set down on a patterned carpet! The owner's beloved rugs looked fantastic once we took down the carpet and polished the floorboards, and they were the first thing you saw when you walked into the room. She was ecstatic by the outcome.

Often, styles from the past are out of trend today, and pelmet-type curtains that collect dust are definitely out of style. When the blinds or white linen curtains are replaced, the entire space appears much larger, allowing more natural light to enter. Dark brown kitchen cabinets have evolved into another fashion statement over time. The entire room can look fantastic by removing the doors and painting them again with special cabinet paint. You must examine the layout of your rooms and determine what elements you like and dislike. It has no place in your house if you don't enjoy it.

Certain locations require extra care. Your kitchen will be a wastebasket. It is criminal how much food the average American home wastes. Large refrigerators provide a lot of hiding areas for meals that have been opened but not eaten within the allotted period. We dispose of items at a startling rate, which is expensive. I'm willing to wager that there are ingredients in your food pantry that you purchased years ago but haven't used or are unlikely to use. You will be happier and won't have to be reminded of your waste every time you open a cupboard if you plan to utilize it or give it to the world's needy instead of throwing it away. We hoard, and while we condemn others who do so on television, we are not all that different from them in that we have a lot of stuff that we do not need and will never use.

The restrooms are another place to check for clutter. Products that promise us eternal youth often win our trust. We like to believe in fantasy even though we know that our skin will never look like a baby's again and that our hair will never be shinier. The issue is that when the bubble bursts, all pricey containers filled with broken promises are left behind to remind us of our conceit. Get rid of them or offer them to someone else so they can try them out without paying for anything.

I can still recall my initial attempt at decluttering my house. The extra items I had in case something went wrong surprised me. The objective is to purchase the greatest quality item possible for your intended usage rather than deprive yourself of anything. You won't need extras in this way. Since technology is constantly evolving and many older cables are no longer functional, I was astounded by the sheer number of cables I discovered hidden away in drawers.

Make sure a room is completed before moving on to the next as you move from one to the other. There is another way to approach this if your thinking is off. Leave all your electronics outside of the room you're working on and dedicate an hour to it. After that, shut the door behind you, take a 30-minute break, and sip some tea or coffee. Then return to it, giving it your whole attention. The room you are working on without distractions. You have been given several hours to complete the decluttering process and will focus on it throughout that period.

Move everything that won't be kept outside into the garage so it won't hinder you, and celebrate your freedom from all that used to occupy that space. You can find yourself rescuing items if you leave plastic bags filled with stuff lying around your house, but there are certain clear guidelines. Does the object make you happy? Does it have a particular function? It vanishes if it doesn't. You can then move on to the next room and be quite content with what you have left behind as you tidy each one and even consider how you may decorate it more minimally. You'll be able to locate items. Your life will be much easier overall, and you won't have to clean up as much. I've spoken with several people whose lives were completely transformed by the decluttering process. They stopped listening to the advertisements since they had all they needed and were content with what they had. Not only that, but many of their worldly friends converted to a minimalist lifestyle after witnessing firsthand how amazing the homes looked and how content the occupants were—many of whom had already made the switch.

Clear Out For A Minimalist

17 Easy Pointers DIRECTIONS TO Declutter Your Home

It seems like everyone wants to get thinner these days. For the majority, retiring to the absolute essentials seems appealing. And for a really good reason.

Reducing clutter is a crucial tactic for leading a simpler life. Possessing and desiring children provides you with emotional stability and the confidence to refuse mindless consumption.

Although decreasing seems simple, many of us find it difficult to incorporate it into our daily lives. It frequently falls into the "I'll do it later" category.

This is due to a few factors.

● You don't think that disclosing is valuable.

● You have no idea where to begin

I will assume that you already recognize the value of decluttering, but you still require some assistance to get started.

First decoder tip: Recover a room

This is one of my all-time favorite deduction techniques from the guys at The Minimalists. The concept is straightforward. Select a room in your home and pack everything into boxes. Remove the contents of the box only when necessary during the following month.

By the end of the month, you will have two piles. One pile includes everything you used, and a second contains everything you didn't.

You can now make decisions quickly by looking back at the things you didn't use and making quick decisions.

Divider tip number two: Use numbers

Depending on your motivations, you may find that counting your achievements is a useful strategy for decreasing them.

I believe it is powerful in certain areas. A good example would be clothes. Knowing I want three high-quality partners in my rotation motivates me.

Aiming for 33 clothing items seemed more appealing than just declaring that you would reduce your waist size.

If you apply this method to everything you do, you risk competing against others for the sake of competing rather than concentrating on the advantages of simplicity.

Trick Number 3: Create Micro-Liĕts: I adore this tip since the lists may be detailed. For example, rather than making a lengthy list of everything you need to declutter around the house, you could make a micro-liĕt of the steps you're going to do to clean out your kitchen cabinets.

Breaking tasks into manageable chunks, like this one, puts you in a situation where you have to settle for fast wins since it might only take thirty minutes to clean your kitchen cabinets.

Divider tip number four: Assign a timer
When it comes to details, you can become lost in the details, so sometimes,

it's best to make snap decisions to keep your momentum going.

It's a great idea to schedule your task to get things moving. It could also be an enjoyable way to involve your family. You could set up a large countdown timer on your smartphone, and everyone would need to sign in to clear the area at that time.

Tip number five for decluttering: Set up an exchange property

This tip suits ladies who own purses full of unique cosmetics.

I realize it's frustrating. You purchased these products expecting great things, only to discover they aren't for you. You hang onto these things, hoping you might change your mind. Feelings of guilt creep in when you convince your partner or lover that this face serum will transform your life.

The truth is that you will never use these products again, yet you cannot bring yourself to throw them away. After everything, you've hardly touched them!

What actions do you take? Throw a swap party for your girlfriends. Simply because the products didn't work for you doesn't mean it won't work for someone else.

Bring all your female friends over for an exchange party. Everyone brings their unique beauty products to exhibit and sample. By the end, hopefully, you will have products you will use, or at the very least, your unique products won't have gone to waste.

You can also do this with your accessories, shoes, and clothes.

Chapter 5: Step 3: Make Your Kitchen And Fridge More Minimalist

You can finish this step as you work on the second step because it is a substep of the prior step. Proceed cautiously with this stage since it's normally challenging to buy less food than you need, particularly if you buy groceries and food weekly or monthly.

Food minimalism is beneficial since it raises your awareness of the value of food and purchases the food items you need. If you immediately rummage through your refrigerator, you might find a few or perhaps many products you haven't used in a long time and others that you've let go bad and decay.

We frequently purchase food products to utilize later. You are walking down an aisle when you spot a packet of pasta and feel compelled to buy it since you are craving pasta. But after a few weeks, you find that you haven't even touched the pasta, and it's still sitting in the kitchen cupboard, useless. I believe you can identify with this situation.

There was a moment in your life when you made a purchase that did not fulfill its intended use and ended up in the garbage. You could have done better with the money you squandered on that buy. You may gradually train yourself to buy only what you need, eat what you buy, and eliminate the impulse to buy things in advance by introducing minimalism into your kitchen and the food you buy and consume.

Here's how to go about doing that.

First, inventory everything you currently own and determine how long each item will endure. Don't buy extra rice right now if the pack you have will last you for a week.

Make a list of the foods you must have right now, and buy enough to last no more than five days. If you don't use an item in that time, you probably won't use it again.

Eat everything you have purchased; get more once you have only enough food for a single day. If there are items in your cupboard or fridge that you don't think go well together, consider finding recipes that will help you put those items together. This will force you to consume what you already own, saving you money and inspiring you to cook in new and inventive ways.

Follow these instructions for a few weeks, then evaluate the outcomes. If you are consuming the food in your cabinets and refrigerator and wasting less, then minimalism is a fantastic fit for you, and you should continue with it. You'll discover that you're enjoying your life more than ever and that it feels much clearer and simpler than it did before.

Not only should you purge unnecessary items from your home to further intensify this emotion, but you should also prioritize introducing no unnecessary items into your home. How to achieve that is covered in the next chapter.

Chapter 3: The Process of Decluttering

Your current residence was most likely the perfect size when you purchased it. It might have appeared to have shrunk gradually. In actuality, though, you have been trying to cram as many belongings as you can into the little space in your house as you have acquired throughout your residence. Nowadays, people don't practice economics. They purchase items without much consideration, and if you take a tour of your house and evaluate the harm, you'll discover that every single room—including the bathroom—can be decluttered, giving you back the area you once considered home.

Let's begin by stating that you should schedule time to complete the decluttering procedure. You will never be able to finish it if you attempt to do it room by room in between other aspects of your life. Therefore, you have a better chance of succeeding if you can take time off work, utilize your vacation time, or even just the weekends. The items you genuinely don't need are what you should be on the lookout for in each space. Items in your closet that you never wear may be waiting to be worn on the day you miraculously drop weight. Tell the truth and throw it away. It's not a motivator. It's making you feel even more disappointed. In the same way, do you need every rug, picture, and piece of décor? Recall that going minimalistic entails getting rid of unnecessary items.

When examining a space, make sure to consider natural light as well as how your draperies block it off. You can optimize the light by changing the draperies. Likewise, you can discover that the furniture you own is too large for the area it occupies; in this case, downsizing is usually a smart move since it frees up a ton of space in your house. That does not imply that you must discard items. To be exact, I would advise you to clear out a place in the garage before going through each room with big plastic bin bags and filling them with everything you no longer need. The labels "Give away," "Sell at a garage sale or on eBay," and "Throw away" ought to be attached to the bags. Furniture can be taken straight to the garage and put in its proper location.

What this procedure accomplishes

If you are serious about this procedure, you must go through every drawer, cupboard, kitchen cabinet, corner, and cranny in the house. In actuality, you simplify your life. Put your dresser's makeup supplies into a tray that fits inside the top drawer. In this manner, cleaning the surface won't require you to raise each item separately. The method produces a great deal of room. Cleaning your rooms becomes simpler as a result. You'll find all the products you bought with the idea that they would make your hair shine, make you seem younger, or simply stuff that you had a doctor prescribe but never used in the bathroom. It's time to make everything simpler.

In a similar vein, there will be expired food in the refrigerator. This is typically caused by too much space, which causes items to be pushed to the back of the refrigerator, hidden from view. A minimalist household will find that they are not purchasing large quantities of food that could spoil. The normal American household wastes a tremendous amount of money. A minimalist lifestyle is one in which you buy fresh food whenever feasible and spend less money because eating chemicals will never make you feel better or happier. Owning things isn't the only aspect of minimalism. It is more about taking responsibility for your life.

Pieces of furniture

It's unnecessary to throw away extra furniture if you have more than you need. You can choose to sell this and use the proceeds to help arrange your house to better fit your minimalist lifestyle. For instance, since pastel hues open up a room, you could want to get rid of all the patterns in your house and stick with them. Another thing you might think about doing is widening the opening that separates your interior from the exterior space. This will help you create an inspiring room that feels larger and incorporates some natural elements. If you live in an area with consistent weather, selling items can help you pay for a patio or covered expansion area. However, if you live in a region with unpredictable weather, the transition will be easier, and you can utilize less ornamental outdoor furniture.

Furnishings can yield significant returns on investment, and an excessive amount of furniture in your home can detract from the minimalist aesthetic you are attempting to embrace. Closed doors and the ability to store items allow for the recommended minimalist furnishings, maintaining the home's tidy lines as you move from one room to the next.

How To Get Out Of Debt

It's unlikely that selling your junk will bring in enough money to pay off your debt. Reducing your spending won't enable you to make significant short-term financial savings. This does not imply that minimalism will not help you manage your debt. The minimalist lifestyle will undoubtedly improve your ability to manage debt.

Consider using debt consolidation if you're repaying several loans. By providing you with enough money to cover the entire principal and interest amount of your loan, this solution aims to simplify the administration of your debt. Your new lender might also reimburse any fines you incur for paying off debt early.

The entire cost of debt consolidation may match or exceed the total cost of the separate repayments. The fact that you pay off one obligation each month—albeit in a slightly higher amount—makes it worthwhile to consider. Additionally, you have to keep in mind one payback schedule. One debt payback item will appear better than two or more while you're tracking your monthly expenses.

Since your application for debt consolidation will be approved, your lender will probably review your financial circumstances. If you have a low credit score, be prepared for a higher interest rate. This grade suggests you could be more dependable, as demonstrated by the missing payments on your record. Additionally, it gets worse if you default on some loans.

Make sure you pay on time to prevent your credit score from declining. You can also haggle over the amount when evaluating your loan application if feasible. At most, 90% of your monthly revenue should go toward it.

Think about taking on part-time work during the repayment period as well. You can work as an online tutor or wait tables at a local café. Offering your services is another option if you're good at fixing things. The idea of selling crafts isn't as high as some people claim. Their creation, promotion, and delivery require significant time and work. Additionally, crafting produces mess.

Concentrate on tasks that only need you to exchange time. Start saving money from your regular and part-time jobs, even while you pay off your obligations. Then, invest some of your funds to generate income with little to no work.

Bringing in Passive Income

These days, you're unlikely to get financial security from a regular job or a startup in less than a year or two. It would help if you diversified your passive revenue streams in addition to trading time. You can make money with this kind of revenue even with minimal effort.

Among those who make passive money are novelists and songwriters. Songwriters are compensated every time their songs are performed live or in ads. Writers receive payment for each book that is sold. Royalties are a name for this category of passive income. Many artists and authors become millionaires by penning popular songs and best-selling books respectively.

There are also options for passive income on the Internet. You can create vlogs or a blog. Every advertisement that appears on your blog earns you money. This benefit allows you to work from anywhere at any time. You don't have to quit your current job to concentrate on this. Even without any money at all, you can get started. All you need is a computer and a phone.

But writing a hit song, book, or blog takes work. And there are just too many dumb songs, books, and blogs out there these days. Talent is no longer required. Leave content development to skilled individuals with the guts to add clutter to the Internet if you are not an expert in anything; practice writing before you try to write and publish a song or book.

Renting real estate is an additional way to generate passive income. You could rent a room or two if all you have is your house. You can also make your vacant business property available for lease. It's simpler to locate possible tenants in peer-to-peer rental communities.

Still, investment is the best option for generating passive income. Purchasing bonds is one of the easier ways to invest your money. You can discuss buying bonds with a bank staff. You are lending money to the source institution when you purchase them. In addition to banks, businesses and the government (via the national treasury) occasionally provide those. After the allotted period, they will return your money plus interest.

By using mutual funds, you can also increase the size of your assets. Investing in these is similar to pooling money with other investors. The money raised is then handled by a fund manager, who uses it to buy stocks, bonds, and other assets. Although it is a beginner-friendly alternative, it necessitates first meeting the proper people.

Another type of investing is stocks. Stock entails owning a portion of a public or private company. However, expect to have little influence over business decisions if you only hold 1% or fewer of the stocks. To begin trading stocks, you must have an investing account. Next, find successful businesses and investigate market trends.

Stocks can be purchased through websites, apps, and brokerage houses. You might already own stocks via a 403b or 401k if you work a regular job. Dividends are the earnings from stocks that you get. You can decide whether to reinvest them or keep them.

You should inquire about the possibility of an investor if someone you know has a successful startup with a promising future. However, exercise caution when giving money to friends and family. For every project you undertake with them, a signed paper should exist. Tell them you need to give it some thought if they were the ones who asked. Next, find out if their venture is feasible. Rather than jeopardizing your finances and relationships, you can say no if the idea is not promising.

Contentment Is the Outcome of Will

In the end, your ability to be happy is a result of your willpower. Take note of the word "power." You don't realize how powerful you are. Although your reality may be predetermined, in the end, you selected it since things would have turned out differently if you hadn't made that decision. Really? Why?

You would find a method. You wouldn't put up with certain things, and certain things will be acceptable. You would have different thoughts, which would cause you to feel differently, which would cause you to act differently. Your reality starts to shift the moment you start working differently.

Happiness is the outcome of your will, and everything depends on where you direct your energy. You have a choice in how happy you are at this moment. You're not forced to do it. It is an expression of your perspective on the circumstances.

You either had the option to make a different decision but chose not to, or you just adopted a particular perspective. No matter how you slice it, this is what you have now. In the end, it's a decision.

The Uncomfortable Realization You'll Ever Experience

You are constantly in charge, which is the most annoying truth. Yes, I am aware of this. It doesn't seem that way. That frustrates you to hear. You might even be taken aback. You are in charge at all times, though. Why?

To put it this way, let me. Your body receives thousands of signals from the outside world every day. The senses of sight, hearing, touch, taste, and smell are all relevant to our discussion. We are discussing the inputs from your senses.

But as you are undoubtedly aware, you only pay attention to a small portion. Put another way; you can only pay attention to a small portion of the hundreds and thousands of inputs you encounter daily. You consider or evaluate only a portion of that fraction; you can only recall a portion of it. Some of those recollections find their way into your identity or personal story. See how this operates, do you?

Although everything may happen automatically, it doesn't. What you choose to notice reflects what matters most to you. Some people are more sensitive to particular things because they have different priorities. Others would ignore those and turn their attention elsewhere.

Interpretation is where this process is most evident. Priorities become apparent when you begin to form opinions about what you see, evaluate it, and conduct an analysis of it. That is the point at which your rights and values are relevant.

Why does this matter so much? That's how you alter reality, then. The key to editing is to pay attention to some details and ignore others. It all comes down to focusing on some aspects and ignoring others.

Your expectations and presumptions influence how you see the world. As a result, your perceptions of the world are either reinforced and strengthened or undermined, and you begin to search for alternative presumptions and expectations.

This has a significant impact because, in the end, you get to choose how you define reality. It all comes down to your perspective, what you choose to emphasize, how you choose to read them, and what you decide to include and exclude.

That's a lot of power, yet the sad truth is that most people let themselves live hopeless, helpless lives confined to invisible prison walls. Imagine being weak, vulnerable, and trapped while you go about your daily life without realizing that you have the key to your mental jail. You are in charge. You are the only one who can free yourself from your inner jail; everything else is a matter of expectation and assumption. It all comes down to decisions.

Ways to Become Minimalists

Decluttering is the first step toward a minimalist lifestyle. Let's examine how you can accomplish that:

Could you put it in writing?

Write a detailed list of why you want a simpler life. Put your frustration with debt collectors in writing. Do you find it bothersome that you don't get to spend much time with your children? Remember to write this down. Are you frequently too anxious and tense to get a good night's sleep? Additionally, could you put it in writing? These are your "whys," which will give you the willpower to endure difficult times.

Establish a clutter-free area.

This one functions wonderfully. The spot could be your nightstand, the kitchen table, a countertop, or just one drawer. Take inspiration from this area to reduce and simplify your life. Extend this zone daily, just a bit, as your fondness for that pure, clear surroundings grows. This method transforms a clutter-free kitchen drawer into a clutter-free kitchen area, which becomes a clutter-free household.

Bring three large grocery store boxes home.

Mark one box as "keep," another as "sell," and a third as "charity." Additionally, you should get a sizable trash can, ideally lined, into which you will place all items that are either too worn out to be utilized or broken and cannot be used. Making the house more spacious is the fundamental objective.

Be Hard on the Things That Aren't in Use

Many items in homes appeal both visually and emotionally. Not everything that appeals to the emotions can be thrown away. But do pose the tricky question regarding how often you return to them. If you have been going over them again, store them somewhere significant. If not, they are as valuable as the other clutter overflowing your space. Emotionally compelling objects are helpful, but you must ensure they maintain your attention.

Increase the Amount of Clear Space

It's up to you to make extra room in your life or house. You have to decide what you can afford to part with and what you want to preserve. It will always be up to you to decide. It's never easy to describe how much relief the appearance of space brings. Greater possibility to accept is correlated with more unoccupied space. Being relieved of the weight of needless items is a relief. It translates to less effort and cleaning. It involves a great deal less stress about things you never gave much thought to in real life. It's a freeing sensation.

www.ingramcontent.com/pod-product-compliance
Lightning Source LLC
Chambersburg PA
CBHW052142110526
44591CB00012B/1820